Choosing a

By Jenny Giles
Illustrated by Isabel Lowe

"Hello, Rachel!   Hello, Sam!"
said Andy.
"Come and see the puppies.
They are here in the basket
with the mother dog."

3

Rachel said,
"Oh look, Sam!
The puppies are asleep."

Dad said,
"Do you see a puppy you like?"

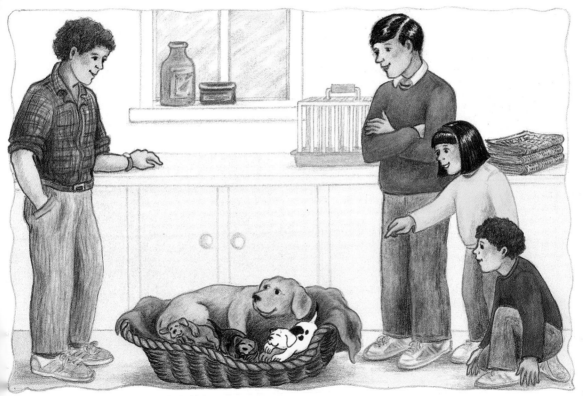

"I like
this little
brown puppy,"
said Rachel.

"I like
this little puppy
with the **spots**,"
said Sam.

"The puppy with the spots
is awake," said Dad.
"Here he comes.   Look, Sam!"

The puppy went
for a little walk.
"Come on, puppy," said Sam.

The puppy sat down.
He looked up at Rachel.

"Oh, look!" said Rachel.
"He **likes** me!
Come on, come to me . . . Spot!"

Spot got up,
and he went
to Rachel and Sam.

"We like **Spot**," said Sam.
"Can he come home with us?"

How to care for your puppy

13

"Yes, he can go home with you today," said Andy.
"He is the biggest puppy."

"Oh, thank you, Andy," said Rachel.

"Come on, Spot," said Sam.
"You are coming home with us."